First published in Great Britain 2003
by Egmont Books Limited
239 Kensington High Street, London W8 6SA
Copyright © Hasbro International Inc. All rights reserved.
Shock Mountain originally published by
Marvel Comics, a division of Panini UK Ltd

ISBN 1 4052 0475 3

1 3 5 7 9 10 8 6 4 2

Printed in Italy

ACTION MAN

SHOCK MOUNTAIN

EGMONT

At Mission Control, Action Man was being debriefed on a new crisis facing mankind. Overnight, an electrical fence had sprung up at the base of Europe's largest mountain. A huge laser was stopping anyone flying in.

"Tempest is behind all this!" said the General. "And he says that unless Dr X is announced ruler of the world, he'll destroy all the major cities!"

Action Man must defeat Tempest and destroy the laser!

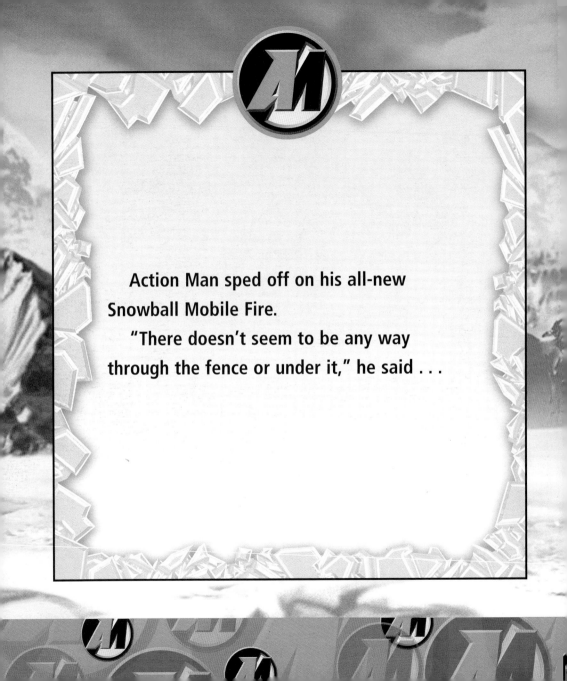

Action Man sped off on his all-new
Snowball Mobile Fire.

"There doesn't seem to be any way
through the fence or under it," he said . . .

. . . "Which leaves only one other route –
to go over it!"

Action Man accelerated hard, and zoomed
off the edge of a cliff, clearing the fence with
inches to spare.

As Action Man sped up the mountain towards Tempest's station, two of Dr X's henchmen suddenly appeared from nowhere.

"Quick, we've gotta stop him!" they shouted.

"Sorry, can't stop," said Action Man. ". . . Not when your boss needs to be fired. And talking of being fired . . ."

Action Man blasted a massive snowball from the Snowball Mobile Fire, knocking the men flying.

Inside the mountain hide-out, Tempest watched Action Man on the closed circuit video-link.

"So, you really think you can defeat me do you, Action Man?" he snarled. "All this mountain air must be affecting your mind. Ha! Ha!"

Action Man switched to stealth mode. "Time to take this baby off-piste and see what it can really do!" he cried.

Action Man zoomed off the track and among the trees. Before long, Tempest's secret station was before him.

"Now to destroy that laser!" Action Man muttered to himself. He hadn't noticed Tempest spying on him through binoculars.

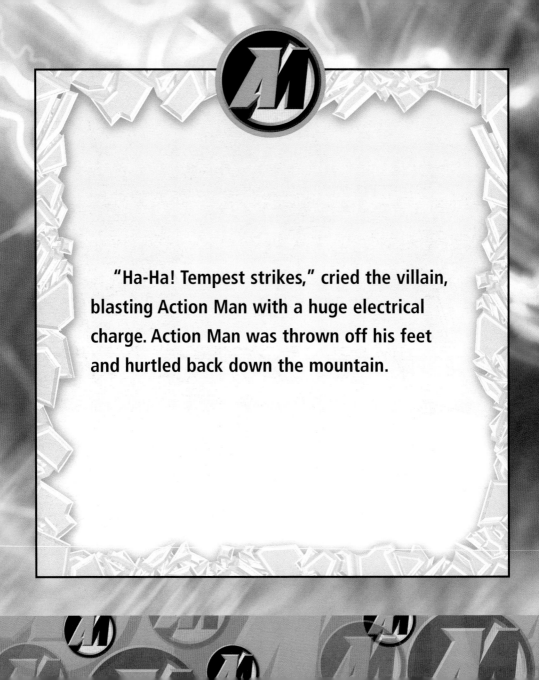

"Ha-Ha! Tempest strikes," cried the villain, blasting Action Man with a huge electrical charge. Action Man was thrown off his feet and hurtled back down the mountain.

Action Man landed with a huge crash, far from the Snowball Mobile Fire.

"I'd be a gonner if it wasn't for this protective suit!" he muttered to himself. "Tempest seems to get stronger every time we meet."

Action Man needed a plan. He had to get back to the Snowball Mobile Fire and find some way of destroying Tempest's operation once and for all.

Suddenly Tempest appeared above him.
"You may as well give up now, Action Man! If I strike you again, you'll never recover. And once I've finished with you, the United Nations will definitely make Dr X ruler of the world! Ha! Ha! Ha!"

"You know I can never let that happen, Tempest! Not while I'm still The Greatest Hero of Them All!" said Action Man.

"But you're snowed under," Tempest replied, with an evil grin. "How are you going to stop me?"

Action Man threw a snowball in Tempest's face, stunning him for a second. But he soon recovered.

"Bar-Ha! You think a snowball is enough to defeat the almighty Tempest?" he cackled. He hadn't noticed that Action Man had managed to get back to the Snowball Mobile Fire.

"Let's see if this knocks some sense into you," shouted Action Man, as the Snowball Mobile Fire launched a huge snowball, straight at Tempest.

Tempest was knocked flying. His lightning bolts crashed into his laser, destroying it once and for all.

"Mission completed!" said Action Man. "The laser has been destroyed, and as for Tempest… well, he's knocked out cold! I've certainly put a stop to his evil plan… until the next time."